Junior Library of Money

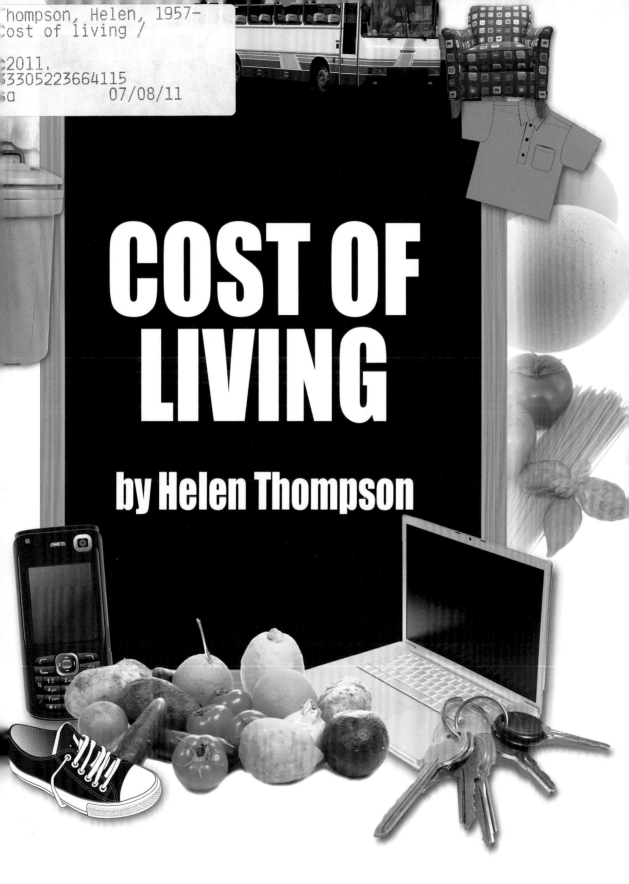

COST OF LIVING

by Helen Thompson

MASON CREST PUBLISHERS INC.
370 Reed Road
Broomall, Pennsylvania 19008
(866)MCP-BOOK (toll free)
www.masoncrest.com

First Printing
9 8 7 6 5 4 3 2 1

Library of Congress Cataloging-in-Publication Data

Thompson, Helen, 1957–
 Cost of living / by Helen Thompson.
    p. cm. — (All about money)
 Includes index.
 ISBN 978-1-4222-1762-7   ISBN 978-1-4222-1759-7 (series)
 ISBN 978-1-4222-1881-5 (pbk.)   ISBN 978-1-4222-1878-5 (pbk. series)
 1. Cost and standard of living—Juvenile literature. 2. Prices—Juvenile literature.
3. Finance, Personal—Juvenile literature. I. Title.
 HD6978.T46 2011
 339.4′2—dc22
                             2010029402

Design by Wendy Arakawa.
Produced by Harding House Publishing Service, Inc.
www.hardinghousepages.com
Cover design by Torque Advertising and Design.
Printed by Bang Printing.

Contents

Introduction

Our lives interact with the global financial system on an almost daily basis: we take money out of an ATM machine, we use a credit card to go shopping at the mall, we write a check to pay the rent, we apply for a loan to buy a new car, we set something aside in a savings account, we hear on the evening news whether the stock market went up or down. These interactions are not just frequent, they are consequential. Deciding whether to attend college, buying a house, or saving enough for retirement, are decisions with large financial implications for almost every household. Even small decisions like using a debit or a credit card become large when made repeatedly over time.

And yet, many people do not understand how to make good financial decisions. They do not understand how inflation works or why it matters. They do not understand the long-run costs of using consumer credit. They do not understand how to assess whether attending college makes sense, or whether or how much money they should borrow to do so. They do not understand the many different ways there are to save and invest their money and which investments make the most sense for them.

And because they do not understand, they make mistakes. They run up balances they cannot afford to repay on their credit card. They drop out of high school and end up unemployed or trying to make ends meet on a minimum wage job, or they borrow so much to

pay for college that they are drowning in debt when they graduate. They don't save enough. They pay high interests rates and fees when lower cost options are available. They don't buy insurance to protect themselves from financial risks. They find themselves declaring bankruptcy, with their homes in foreclosure.

We can do better. We must do better. In an increasingly sophisticated financial world, everyone needs a basic knowledge of our financial system. The books in this series provide just such a foundation. The series has individual books devoted specifically to the financial decisions most relevant to children: work, school, and spending money. Other books in the series introduce students to the key institutions of our financial system: money, banks, the stock market, the Federal Reserve, the FDIC. Collectively they teach basic financial concepts: inflation, interest rates, compounding, risk vs. reward, credit ratings, stock ownership, capitalism. They explain how basic financial transactions work: how to write a check, how to balance a checking account, what it means to borrow money. And they provide a brief history of our financial system, tracing how we got where we are today.

There are benefits to all of us of having today's children more financially literate. First, if we can help the students of today start making wise financial choices when they are young, they can hopefully avoid the financial mishaps that have been so much in the news of late. Second, as the financial crisis of 2007–2010 has shown, poor individual financial choices can sometimes have implications for the health of the overall financial system, something that affects everyone. Finally, the financial system is an important part of our overall economy. The students of today are the business and political leaders of tomorrow. We need financially literate citizens to choose the leaders who will guide our economy through the inevitable changes that lie ahead.

Brigitte Madrian, Ph.D.
Aetna Professor of Public
Policy and Corporate Management
Harvard Kennedy School

What Do You Need to Live?

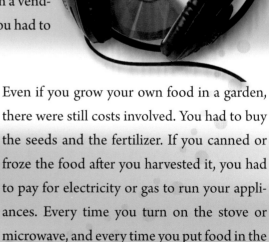

Every day, you probably spend money (or your parents do). Almost everything we do costs something!

Think about it.

Every time you eat a meal or a snack, the food costs money. It doesn't matter whether you go out to eat at a restaurant, buy a candy bar from a vending machine, or cook a meal at home—you had to spend money.

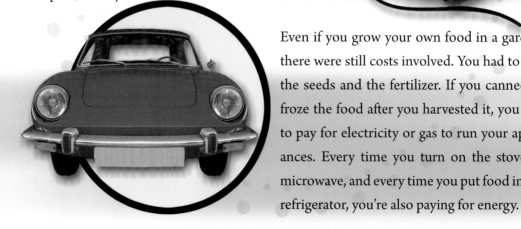

Even if you grow your own food in a garden, there were still costs involved. You had to buy the seeds and the fertilizer. If you canned or froze the food after you harvested it, you had to pay for electricity or gas to run your appliances. Every time you turn on the stove or microwave, and every time you put food in the refrigerator, you're also paying for energy.

The same thing is true when it comes to going places. We need to be able to get from place to place for a variety of reasons. In the twenty-first century, most of us need to drive or take a bus or a train to get to our jobs. (Though a few of us may walk or ride a bicycle.) We drive or ride on public transportation to visit friends, to go out to have a good time, or to go shopping. When we go on vacations, we might drive—or we might fly. And all those things cost money.

Just having a place to live costs money. Most people either pay rent or make mortgage payments. If they own their own homes or live with family or friends, keeping a house warm and lit still costs money. Repairs, decorating, and insurance are other costs that come with having a place to live.

When you come right down to it, pretty much everything in life costs money. Your clothes cost money. (Even if you sew them yourself, you still have to buy fabric and thread.) Cosmetics and things like shampoo and toothpaste aren't free either.

Look around your house. You probably see things like books, electronics, knickknacks, furniture ... stuff! And it all cost money. When people talk about the "cost of living," they mean all the things you spend money on during ordinary daily life.

How Much Does It Cost to Live?

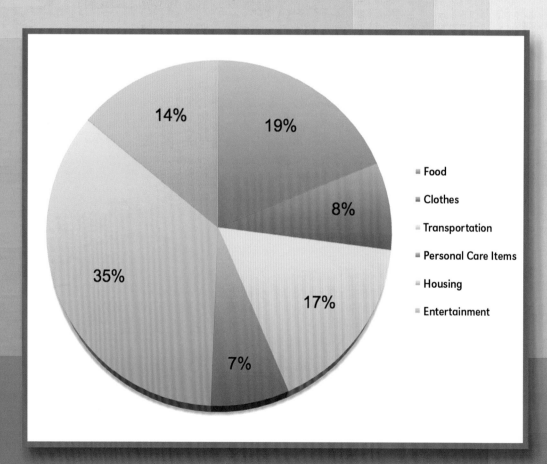

- Food
- Clothes
- Transportation
- Personal Care Items
- Housing
- Entertainment

19%

8%

17%

7%

35%

14%

Money experts have come up with the percentages that almost everyone usually spends on various things in life, like food and clothes and housing. These percentages are shown in the pie graph on the opposite page.

As you can see, housing is the most expense piece of the "pie." Next is food, and then transportion. Of course some people will spend more on housing than others, or others will spend less on entertainment. Some people might spend lots more on clothes, or they might walk to work and spend next to nothing on transporation. Every household is a little different. This graph just shows the average numbers.

You'll notice the total is less than 100 percent. This is because most people don't spend ALL their money on daily life. They might also put money away for vacations—or into a savings account for their children's education. Some people who don't have insurance may spend a lot on medical expenses. So there are lots of variables involved.

OUT ON YOUR OWN

As a little kid, you probably weren't very aware of how much things cost. The grownups in your life took care of all that. But that's changing now.

The older you get, the more you'll be expected to handle your own money. You've probably already started paying for some of the things you use in your life. And when the time comes for you to move out and be on your own, you're going to need to understand the cost of living—and how to pay for it!

The Cost of Having a Place to Live

When you first move out on your own, you'll probably rent an apartment. This is how most people start out life.

So you'll probably check the newspapers to find apartments that are available. Or you might go online to check craigslist for your area. You could also ask friends and family if they know of any place you could rent.

How much these apartments cost will depend on a bunch of different things, like how big the apartment is and where it's located. One of the big factors that affect rent costs is the region where you live. Rent in some parts of the country is much cheaper than in others. So you might be able to get a very nice apartment in a small town in the Midwest for under $500—but you'll probably find it difficult to find even a tiny apartment for rent in New York City for less than $1000.

What Are the
HIDDEN COSTS?

So say you've found what looks like the perfect apartment for you, and the rent seems like something you can afford. Keep in mind that you'll probably have to pay a security deposit as well. This is money that the landlord keeps for as long as you live in the apartment. When you move out, if everything is in the same shape as when you moved in, you'll get that money back—but if you've damaged anything, the landlord will deduct the cost of repairs from the security deposit. Some landlords will also want you to pay an extra month's rent at the beginning, to be sure you won't move out without paying your last month's rent. All this means that you'll probably need up to 3 times the cost of one month's rent in order to move in.

There are also lots of costs involved with having your own house that may not have occurred to you. Here are some examples:

• furniture

You'll need a bed, something to sit on, a table, maybe a desk. Friends and family may be able to give you some of these, or you can buy them more cheaply from a second-hand store.

• cleaning supplies and other household items

Hopefully, you're going to want to keep your apartment at least a little clean! You'll need things like a broom, a vacuum cleaner, cleaning supplies, garbage cans, etc.

• decorations and linens

Maybe it won't be all that important to you to make your house look nice, but you're going to at least need bedding, towels, and curtains or blinds for privacy.

• utilities

This is a big one. Unless your rent includes these costs, you're going to need to pay for both heat and electricity. You may also need to pay for water and garbage collection.

THE COST OF EATING

How much you spend on food will vary, depending on what and where you eat. If you eat out (even at fast-food restaurants), you'll end up spending lots more than you would if you ate at home. So if you have a limited number of dollars to spend every week, a good way to save money is to eat at home.

Once you make that decision, there are still other variables that will affect how much you spend on the food you eat. Some kinds of food are more expensive than others.

These foods are cheap and nutritious, so they're a good way to fill up if you're trying to save money:
• pasta
• all kinds of beans
• cereal
• bread
• peanut butter

These foods cost a little more, but your mother will want you to eat them in order to stay healthy:
• fresh fruits and vegetables

The most expensive food?
• meat
If you eat less meat, you'll save money. You can get at least some of your protein from other cheaper foods, including beans and peanut butter.

Sainsbury's
THICK CUT
ORANGE MARMALADE
with Ginger
Made from Seville Orange
454 gram

What Are the HIDDEN COSTS?

When you think about how much money you have to spend on food, you need to be aware that there are also other costs involved that go along with eating. Some of these are more obvious than others, but you need to remember to include them when you're planning how much money you have available to spend during a month.

For example, if you go out to eat, the cost of the food isn't the only expense; you also need to remember to include the cost of the gas or bus ride to get to the restaurant. And if you eat at home, there are also a few hidden costs, especially when you're first setting up your own living arrangements.

If you're just starting to live on your own, here are some smaller items you'll need to buy (and then replace as they wear out or get used up):

- dish washing soap or dishwasher detergent
- cooking utensils (like wooden spoons and spatulas)
- sponges or dishcloths and dish towels
- can opener
- plastic wrap and aluminum foil
- basic staples like salt and pepper, sugar, and coffee or tea

Here are some more expensive items you'll also need:
- dishes for eating on
- spoons, forks, and knives for eating
- sharper knives for cooking
- pots and pans

If your apartment doesn't come with these, you may also need these expensive appliances:
- a stove and a refrigerator

(a microwave & dishwasher are nice but not necessary)

THE COST OF WEARING CLOTHES

When you get out on your own, you may be surprised by how much you end up spending on clothes. Especially if you're working, you may need more formal clothing items and shoes, attire that is appropriate for your work. You'll still want informal clothes, like blue jeans and T-shirts. And then you'll need shoes for each season of the year—boots and warm coats for winter (especially if you live somewhere cold during the winter months) and swimming suits, shorts, and sandals for the summer.

Here are the items of clothing you'll probably need to purchase each year.

- 7–9 outfits appropriate for your work (if you're a male, this will mean 7–9 dress shirts, with 3 or 4 pairs of dress pants). Depending on where you live, you may need different outfits for summer and winter.
- 2–3 pairs of jeans or casual pants
- 5–7 casual sweaters or sweatshirts (same number of T-shirts for summer)
- 2–3 dress shoes
- 1–2 pairs of sneakers or casual shoes (you may want sandals for summer as well)
- 7 sets of underwear
- at least 7 pairs of socks
- seasonal clothing like winter coats, gloves, and bathing suits

You can check out how much each item will cost online to determine the amount of money you're likely to spend on clothes in a year. (Of course, some people spend a lot more on clothes, but this should be enough for you to get by!)

What Are the Hidden Costs?

If you make a list of all the clothes you'll need to buy in a year, based on the list provided on the previous page, odds are it will add up to at least $1,000. So that you don't have to handle that all at once, you might want to break up that cost by setting aside about $80 to $100 each month for your clothing expenses.

But those expenses are only a piece of what you're going to have to pay for the privilege of wearing clothes! In addition to the cost of buying the clothes you wear, you'll also have to pay to keep them looking good. For the most part, this means keeping your clothes clean and repairing clothes that have been damaged.

One of the most significant hidden costs of owning and wearing clothes is cleaning them. Depending on where you live, you may or may not have a washing machine and dryer in your apartment building, dormatory, or house.

Many people who don't have a washer or dryer get their laundry done at laundromats, businesses that have many washing machines and dryers that you can pay to use. The cost of washing your clothes each week at a laundromat can add up over time, even when it only costs a few dollars to wash a single load. If you have many clothes, it may cost more, since you'll need to do more than one load of laundry at once.

Laundry detergent and dryer sheets are also part of the cost of doing laundry. Even if you have a washer or dryer at your place, you will need to pay the cost of the power and water that your washer and dryer use.

If you damage or soil your clothes in a way you can't take care of on your own—stain your best suit, for example—you'll need to have it dry cleaned professionally, adding to the cost of owning your clothes. (Most clothes that are dry-clean only should be cleaned at least once a year, if not more.)

The Cost of Getting Places

No matter where you live, no matter how you get around, you'll have to pay to travel from place to place. Whether using public transportation (like a bus or subway system), traveling by taxi, or using your own car, going places costs money.

Let's say you're trying to get from your house to the mall. You've got a lot of choices as to how you get there, and each has its own costs.

You could take the bus, often the cheapest way to get where you want to go. Most bus systems cost very little to take a single ride, and in some places, students can use the bus system without paying if they use show their student ID card. Remember, though, the bus can take a long time. You don't have control over when the bus stops and when it arrives. In many cases, taking the bus costs much more in time than it does in actual money.

A quicker option would be to take a taxi to the mall. In a cab you'll have control over the stops you make (if you make any), but you'll pay much more than you would taking the bus. Most taxis charge by the distance traveled, adding onto a base charge for using the taxi in the first place. You might get to the mall faster, but you'll always pay more for a cab than a bus ticket.

Traveling further than the mall? To your grandma's house on the other side of the country? Take a plane and you'll arrive in a very short amount of time, but you'll pay a lot for the ticket there and back. Take a bus or train and you'll pay less, but getting there could take more than a full day.

WHAT ARE THE HIDDEN COSTS?

Proposal No. PC 2495

AIG Kenya Insurance Co. Ltd.
A member of American International Group, Inc

PROPOSAL FOR PRIVATE CAR INSURANCE

SECTION A   PERSONAL / CORPORATE DATA

PIN No.

Applicant)   Other Name:_____ Occupation:_____

(yy)_____ ID/Passport No._____

PIN No.

Position:_____

Town:_____

eet:_____

e Phone:_____

			Seating capacity including driver	Registered letters and numbers	Engine and chassis numbers

☐ Duty Free
☐ Duty Free

Paid

h the declaration below: ⁀ DUTY FREE basis and

So, you're tired of taking the bus or paying high prices for taxi cabs, and you think getting a car is the solution to your travel problems. Owning a car can be a great help, making it easy to travel where you want, whenever you want. You don't have to rely on bus schedules or getting the attention of a cab driver—but what are the hidden costs to owning a car?

First, you'll have to keep gas in your car at all times in order to use it. The price of gas changes often, which can make this cost hard to estimate. Each car is slightly different too, meaning you may pay a different amount for a tank of gas than a friend with a smaller car. Larger cars use gas more quickly too, which means you'll need to pay for more gas to go the same distance. If you own a car, you'll also have to pay for car **insurance**, to protect you if you're in an accident or your car is damaged. Insurance can cost a lot, especially if you're young and male. (Young men usually pay higher insurance rates because of statistics showing that these drivers are involved in more accidents on average.) Finally, if you're car is damaged in any way, or if parts of it wear out, you'll have to pay for repairs, the costs of which vary.

TAKING CARE OF YOURSELF

Taking good care of yourself is a part of growing up and being responsible. You need your health (whether physical, mental, or emotional) in order to function in life. Like so many other aspects of life, caring for yourself will cost you money.

Let's say you're sick, for example. If it were a cold or flu, you might know to get some rest, drink plenty of water, and spend a few days recovering, but what if you weren't sure what you had and needed to go to see the doctor? That will cost money. Paying your doctor can be done in a few different ways. In many cases, if you have health insurance, your insurance company will take care of paying the doctor.

Of course, you pay for health insurance, so technically, you're paying at least part of the cost of seeing the doctor. If you don't have insurance, you'll have to pay for your doctor "out of pocket," meaning all on your own. Let's say your doctor knows exactly what's wrong with you and can give you medicine so that you'll get better. That medicine will cost you too, though insurance can help pay for that as well. In general, any medical examination and treatment costs money.

What Are the HIDDEN COSTS?

Beyond the costs of seeing doctors and buying medicine, taking care of yourself also means making sure you don't have to make an emergency visit to your doctor, dentist, or worse, to the hospital. The hidden costs of taking care of yourself often come from buying small items you might take for granted, the kinds of items that you use everyday. Brushing your teeth, keeping yourself clean, and treating minor medical problems with items you can buy at your local drugstore or supermarket are all part of responsibly caring for your own health and well-being. Taking care of yourself can also mean making sure you look your best, perhaps buying and wearing makeup or other cosmetic items.

Here's a list of some of the most common self-care items. Once you're out on your own, you'll need to keep these things on hand.

- toothbrush and toothpaste
- razor, razorblades, and shaving cream
- makeup and other cosmetic items
- hairbrush, shampoo, conditioner, and other hair products
- over-the-counter medicines such as those for a cold, headache, or stomach pain
- band-aids and other small medical items (such as anti-bacterial cream)
- skin-care products (like mosturizers and sanitizers)
- sanitary products (if you're a woman)

Buying these items is part of taking care of yourself. The costs of these things are in addition to the costs of going to the doctor, dentist, or hospital.

The Cost of Having a Good Time

You might think that, of all things, having fun should be free. While feeling good doesn't cost anything, the way you get that good feeling might cost you more than you think. Consider your favorite activities, the things you love to do with your friends or on your own when you've got some free time. How much do these things cost?

Do you like going to concerts? Concert tickets cost money, as do the CDs you buy from the merchandise stand after the show. Is reading your thing? So much so that you read a new book every week? Those books will cost you (unless they're taken out from your local library, of course). No matter what you love to do, it's almost a guarantee that at some point you're paying some money to enjoy those items or activities.

Some of the most common ways to entertain yourself all cost money. Here are some of the pricier items. These are usually the sort of investment you only need to make once or once every few years.

• television
• mp3 player or iPod
• computer
• musical instruments

Here are some cheaper forms of entertainment—but these are expenses you're likely to put out every week or two.

• movies
• books & magazines
• music downloads
• sports events

As you look at this list, which ones do you feel you NEED? How much do they cost? Add up this amount to reach the number you can expect to pay out for entertainment. You might want to consider some forms of free entertainment too!

What Are the Hidden Costs?

Depending on the kinds of things you like to do in your free time for entertainment, the hidden costs of your favorite activities can vary widely. You may know exactly how much your movie ticket costs, exactly how much you want to spend on a night at a concert—but what about the cost of getting to the theater or concert hall? You may have the costs of your television and cable service accounted for, but what about the cost of the power you're using to watch the TV? Beyond the cost of paying for your entertainment in a direct way (your tickets or television and cable, for example), you'll often pay for the entertainment you enjoy in many ways that can be considered indirect, or secondary.

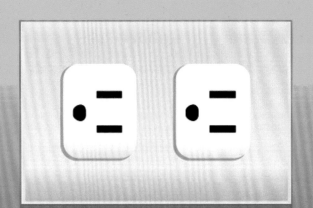

Let's say you plan on going out to dinner with some friends and then you're going to head back to your house to watch television and movies together. You might immediately think of the cost of dinner as being the most significant spending you're going to be doing that night, and for the most part, you'd be right.

But in addition to the cost of the food you eat with your friends, you'll have to get to the restaurant. If you take your car, you'll be spending money on gas. Take a cab and you'll have to pay for that. Go with enough friends and you'll need to take two cars or two cabs, increasing the overall cost of your transportation for the night.

You might have already paid for the movies you're going to watch, perhaps renting them rather than buying to save on money, but you'll also have to pay for the amount of electricity that your television uses while you're watching movies.

This doesn't mean you shouldn't spend your money on having a good time—but you do need to know exactly how much you're really spending. Otherwise, you may find yourself coming up short when it comes time to pay!

The Cost of Communicating with Others

Today's world is more connected than ever before, each of us able to communicate with our friends and loved ones at speeds that people couldn't imagine just a few years ago. E-mail, text messages, cell phones, and instant messaging have all changed the way that people communicate. All of us communicate with each other more often and in many more ways than people have in the past. And that's great.

But each new method of communication costs something.

Staying in touch with your friends and family can become expensive very quickly when you add up all of the costs.

Do you use your cell phone to text and make calls? Not only did the cell phone itself cost money, but so does paying for the service that allows you to make those calls and send those texts. Some cell phone service plans charge by the individual text message, while others allow you to buy a set amount of texts you use each month. It pays to shop around and get the cheapest plan possible.

If you use your computer to chat with your friends while browsing the Internet, in some ways that's a cheaper option for communication—except that the computer itself costs more than a cell phone. Internet service also costs money. Rates vary, depending on the kind of service you have. Again, shop around and get the cheapest service that will give you what you need.

What Other Costs Are There in Life?

You know about many of the key costs you'll need to think about as you grow up and begin to pay for your own clothing, medical care, transportation, and housing, but still other costs are part of living. These include things you can plan for—like going to college or graduate school—and things that you might have a hard time predicting right now, like marriage or the death of a loved one. Still, these costs are part of living just as much as the daily spending you'll do on essential items like food, housing, and transportation. It can seem overwhelming at times—it seems as though EVERYTHING costs money—but understanding the various costs of living can help you prepare for them, rather than leave you **vulnerable** to the unpleasant surprise of a huge bill or large expense you weren't expecting.

In loving memory of

Here are some of the common "extra" expenses that come along in life:

- travel
- hobbies
- birthday gifts and other gifts
- jewelry
- special occasions that require specific clothes or foods
- education at the college or post-graduate level
  - marriage
  - having children
  - cemetery plots and gravestones

Why Does the Cost of Living Go Up?

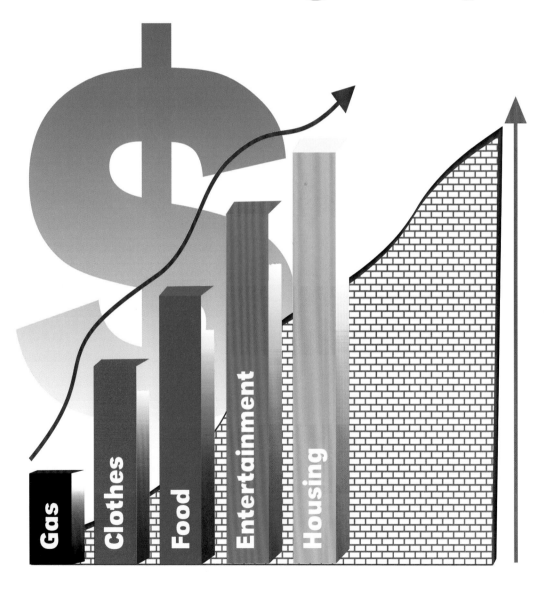

Gas

Clothes

Food

Entertainment

Housing

You may notice that over time, the prices of the items you buy go up. Think of the cost of a movie ticket. Today the average movie ticket costs almost ten dollars. Ten years ago, that ticket cost much less, around five or six dollars. Thirty years ago, it cost about three dollars. And it's not just movie tickets that cost more over time. The price of each and every product and service goes up each year, meaning that the overall cost of living goes up as well. Whether you're paying for gas, clothes, food, entertainment, or housing, you're spending more today than you would have in previous years.

The rise in prices is spread over a long enough period of time that you might not even notice it happening. Over the course of a year, or several years, however, the rise in prices becomes apparent.

Why do prices rise in the way that they do?

Because of something called inflation.

WHAT IS INFLATION?

Inflation causes the prices of products and services to rise. This is because the value of a single dollar decreases each year. This means that ten years from now, you will be able to buy less with a dollar than you can today—and it means that products and services you purchase will cost more. This decrease in a dollar's worth is referred to as a decline in the "purchasing power" of each dollar, meaning the amount you can buy with the same amount of money becomes less.

The rate of inflation—that is, the amount that prices increase—varies slightly, but the average has historically stayed around 4 percent per year. This means that if a product

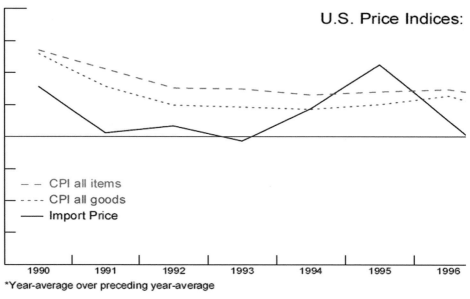

U.S. Price Indices:

- - CPI all items
---- CPI all goods
— Import Price

1990   1991   1992   1993   1994   1995   1996

*Year-average over preceding year-average

cost a dollar at the beginning of the year, by the end of the year, it will probably cost $1.04. This might seem like a very small amount, but when you apply that same rate of increase over ten years, it turns into a 40 percent increase. So buying a soda might cost you a single dollar today, but in a decade, that same soda could cost you $1.40 (as long as inflation stays at the same levels it has historically).

The Increasing Oil Price

Past   Present   Future

All products and services, no matter what they are, are subject to inflation. Likewise, due to inflation, all money loses it's value little by little each year. As strange as it seems, inflation is essentially a natural **economic phenomenon**.

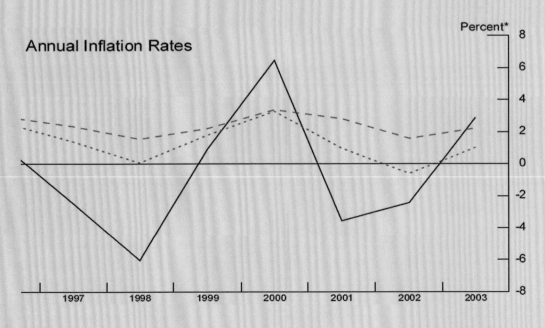

Annual Inflation Rates

The History of Inflation

Inflation—the increase in prices and decrease in the value of money—has been a part of the financial lives of people for centuries. The way we understand inflation today, however, is very different from the understanding that people in the past had of inflation. In fact, the word "inflation" has historically been used not to refer to the increase in prices and the decrease in the value of money, but instead to refer to what we today call "**monetary** inflation."

Monetary inflation is the increase in the amount of money in **circulation** (in use in the economy). In many cases, if too much money is floating around a country, the cost of products and services will increase as well. This happened in the South, for example, during the Civil War, when the Confederacy printed too much money. There was more paper money in circulation than the government could back up with gold.

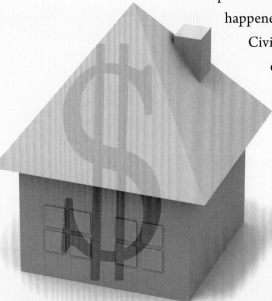

Today, we use the word inflation to refer to price inflation, the increase in the price of products. It's not caused by the government printing too much paper money.

Even how much the President of the United States is paid each year has changed as a result of inflation. President George Washington, the first President of the United States, made just $25,000 each year he was in office. Today, President Barack Obama makes $400,000 a year (though the buying power of his salary is actually much less than Washington's $25,000).

During the Second World War, you could buy a loaf of bread for just fifteen cents, a fraction of what the same kind of bread would cost in a supermarket today.

In the 1930s, the average car cost less than $1000. By comparison, today's cars cost anywhere from $10,000 to several tens of thousands.

WHAT IS THE CONSUMER PRICE INDEX?

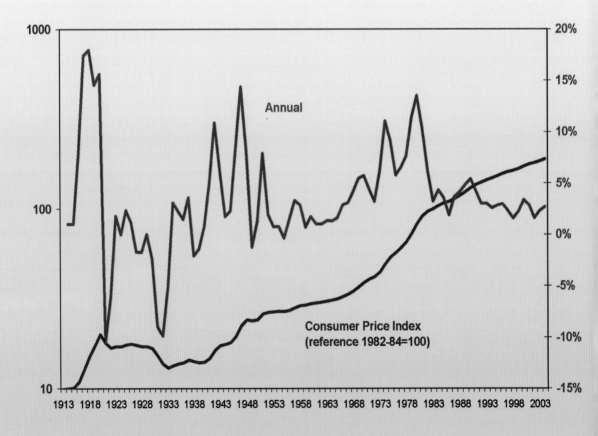

Annual

Consumer Price Index
(reference 1982-84=100)

The Consumer Price Index (also called CPI) is one of many **indices** that measure the cost of living for the average American citizen.

It measures the price of a set number of household items (such as food and other items that are the most commonly bought by American households). This set of items is called a "market basket" or a "consumer basket." The market basket analyzed in the Consumer Price Index is based on several products commonly bought in urban areas around the country. The CPI tracks change in the prices of this market basket by measuring the percentage of their income families are spending on the products in the basket.

The United States Department of Labor's Bureau of Labor Statistics (BLS) has tracked the Consumer Price Index since 1919. The CPI has been measured every month since that time, and is released at the end of each month by the BLS.

The Consumer Price Index doesn't necessarily measure the exact price of goods. Instead, the CPI is a measurement of increases in the cost of living. In effect, the Consumer Price Index indicates one aspect of inflation: how prices have increased in relation to the purchasing power of American families. The CPI only measures common household goods, however, so in many ways it isn't a complete assessment of national inflation or cost of living. The BLS doesn't include what are called investment items in the Consumer Price Index, items such as houses, company stocks, savings bonds, or insurance.

Differences in the Cost of Living

The cost of living goes up and down, depending on a whole bunch of things. Where you live is one of those things. If you live in a major American city—Los Angeles, New York, or Chicago, for example—you'll pay much more for most products and services than you would pay for the exact same products and services in a smaller city or rural area. Since the cost of items and services is much higher in cities than it is in areas outside of cities, the cost of living is higher as a whole.

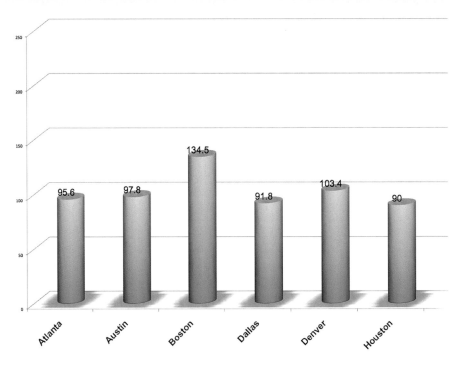

In order to make up for the higher cost of living in urban areas (as compared to rural areas), people who live and work in cities usually make more than workers in areas with a lower cost of living. In most cases, the amount of money you earn at your job, no matter what you do or whether you're paid salary or hourly, will be in proportion to the amount of money it costs to live in your area. If the cost of living is higher, pay for workers usually is higher as well. In some cases, pay may be raised to account for increases in the cost of living.

Sometimes, this doesn't work out, though. Remember, that although you may make more money in a city, you'll also be paying more for almost everything you buy, whether it's food, transportation, or housing. So if you move from a rural area to an urban one to take a better-paying job, you probably won't be pocketing the extra money!

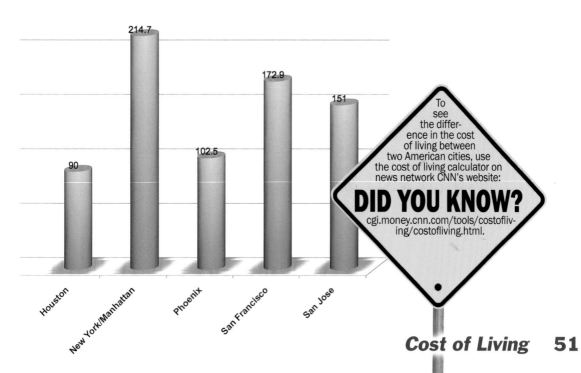

To see the difference in the cost of living between two American cities, use the cost of living calculator on news network CNN's website:

DID YOU KNOW?

cgi.money.cnn.com/tools/costofliving/costofliving.html.

How Does the
GOVERNMENT
Get Involved?

Why does the government keep track of the Consumer Price Index (a measurement of the cost of living in urban areas)? The government has to make sure that it takes into account how much it costs to live so that it can adjust benefits such as Social Security payments and minimum wage. If people's incomes don't keep up with the cost of living, more and more people will drop below the poverty line.

The U.S. government provides a variety of what are called "social services" to the American people. Most social services programs are designed to help people pay for some of their living costs. These services are meant for people who have lost their jobs, the elderly, and people living in poverty.

The taxes that each American pays are what pays for these programs. When you get a paycheck and see that a small percentage of your earnings went to Social Security, you are paying for the payments you will receive when you reach the age of 65 (although that money may be used for others in the meantime). Each of us must pay into these systems so that we may all benefit from them.

But if it costs more to live this year than it did last year because of inflation, the government increases Social Security payments to account for that growth in living costs. Social services aren't meant to pay for all a person's costs of living, but they ARE meant to assist people who may have difficulty paying for their living costs.

The Consumer Price Index is also an indication of the success or failure of the Federal Reserve, the U.S. government's bank, to set economic policies that keep inflation in check. If the CPI shows a huge increase in the cost of living, then too much money is in the economy, leading to inflation. Then the Federal Reserve must correct this problem.

Learn more about what the Federal Reserve does to assist the U.S. economy and keep inflation in check at

DID YOU KNOW?

www.federalreserveeducation.org.

What Does It All Mean to You?

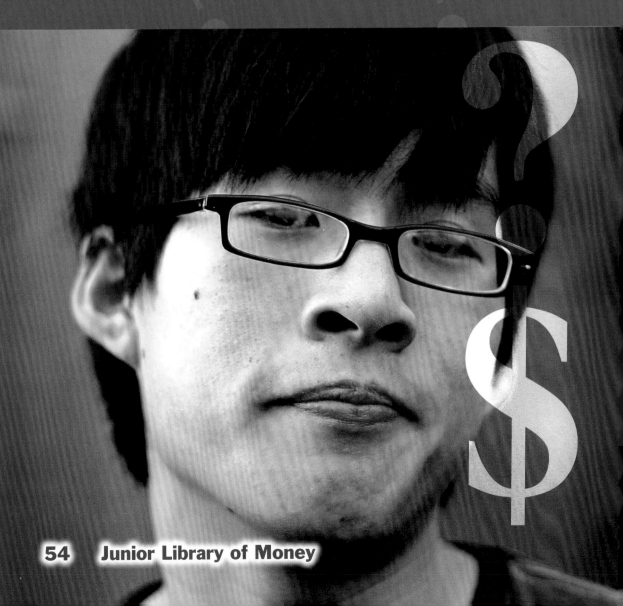

So why should you care about the cost of living?

Knowing about the costs of housing, food, entertainment, communication, and transportation can help you plan your future. In addition, understanding the many hidden costs of each of these kinds of items, including paying for utilities like electricity and the investments you'll need to make to maintain the things you buy, can help you make wise spending choices. If you know that a night at the movies can cost more than the ticket price (after adding in transportation, food and drinks, for example), you might instead choose to spend a night in, giving you extra money to spend on things you want more.

Understanding how money works seems like a lot of work—but money will help you get what you want in life. The more you understand how money works, the more you'll be able to achieve the goals that are important to you.

You'll be out on your own soon. If you understand the cost of living, you'll be ahead of the game—ready to work toward the things that are most important to you!

Here's What
You Need to Remember

- The cost of living is the amount of money a person needs to spend on housing, food, transportation, clothing, and other items that they need to live. Cost of living isn't an exact amount of money, and doesn't mean that's all the money a person needs to live the way he wants, but rather it is a term referring to the amount of money you spend throughout your daily life.

- To get a sense of your cost of living you must consider how much you spend on housing, food, clothing, transportation, entertainment, medical care, and a wide variety of other costs. The amount you spend on each of these categories is factored into your cost of living.

- The cost of living isn't a set amount of money that each person needs to live. It can go up and down based on the conditions in the economy, and depending on where you live. Living in a city typically costs more than living in rural areas, for instance.

Words You Need to Know

circulation: Moving something from place to place or person to person.

economic: Relating to the making and distribution of money, goods, and services.

indices: Things that point to a certain value.

indirect: Not straight-forward.

inflation: A rise in the amount of money available, when the price of various things goes up to meet this increase in money, but the value of the things themselves doesn't change.

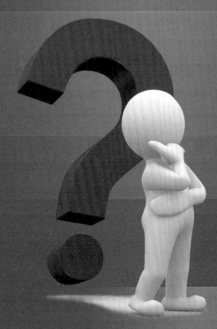

insurance: Monetary protection against unforeseen accidents or disasters.

monetary: Having to do with money or how it moves about in an economy.

phenomenon: Facts or events that can be watched and observed using your senses (rather than deduced with your mind).

policies: Plans or rules that the government or other organizations set in place to help with the running of things.

poverty line: The level of income below which a family is considered officially "poor" by government standards.

variables: Things that change in one way or another so they are difficult to predict.

vulnerable: Being open to injury or attack.

Further Reading

Allman, Barbara. *Banking*. Minneapolis, Minn.: Lerner, 2006.

Butler, Tamsen. *The Complete Guide to Personal Finance: For Teenagers and College Students*. Ocala, Fla.: Atlantic Publishing Group, 2010.

Casu, Barbara, Claudia Girardone, and Philip Molyneux. *Introduction to Banking.* Upper Saddle River, N.J.: Prentice Hall, 2006.

Fowles, Debby. *1000 Best Smart Money Secrets for Students.* Naperville, Ill.: Sourcebooks, Inc., 2005.

Peterson, Judy Monroe. *First Budget Smarts.* New York: Rosen Publishing, 2007.

Wagner, Michael J. *Your Money, Day One: How to Start Right and End Rich.* Charleston, S.C.: BookSurge Publishing, 2009.

Find Out More on the Internet

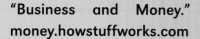

"Business and Money." Howstuffworks.
money.howstuffworks.com

"Cost of Living: Compare Prices in Two Cities." CNN Money.
cgi.money.cnn.com/tools/costofliving/costofliving.html

"Five Money-Saving Shopping Tips." Investopedia.com.
www.investopedia.com/articles/pf/07/five-saving-tips.asp

"Fun Facts About Money." Federal Reserve Bank of San Francico.
www.frbsf.org/federalreserve/money/funfacts.html

MyMoney
 www.mymoney.gov

Young Money Magazine.
www.youngmoney.com

The websites listed on this page were active at the time of publication. The publisher is not responsible for websites that have changed their address or discontinued operation since the date of publication. The publisher will review and update the websites upon each reprint.

Index

Photo Credits

About the Author and Consultant

Helen Thompson lives in upstate New York. She worked first as a social worker and then became a teacher as her second career. She taught money management skills to students in grades seven and eight for several years.

Brigitte Madrian is Professor of Public Policy and Corporate Management in the Aetna Chair at Harvard University's Kennedy School of Government. She has also been on the faculty at the Wharton School and the University of Chicago. She is also a Research Associate at the National Bureau of Economic Research and coeditor of the *Journal of Human Resources*. She is the first-place recipient of the National Academy of Social Insurance Dissertation Prize and the TIAA-CREF Paul A. Samuelson Award for Scholarly Research on Lifelong Financial Security.